What people are saying about ...

Blossoming in Provence

"If Kristin's first book, *Words in a French Life*, planted the seeds of an eclectic and lively French vocabulary in our brains, *Blossoming in Provence* is a full-blown rose of a book made up of lovely, touching, and intimate stories of her life in France. There are even a few thorns thrown in to make us think. One wishes that we could all know these flamboyant, eccentric and lovable characters throughout our lives. And if there is another book, we just might have our wishes granted."

SUZANNE DUNAWAY, Author of *Rome, At Home*

"Kristin has a rare combination of talents for a writer: an artist's ability to see life's unfolding images not only for their external "reality," but also for their inner beauty and symmetry; a philosopher's ability to draw lessons from day-to-day life and apply them to her on-going struggle to grow as a person; and a poet's ability to recognize and express her feelings—often humorously, always honestly. When these abilities are coupled with a talent for weaving a good story that gives us a unique window on French life and language and seldom fails to touch the heart, the result is always a joy to read."

CHARLES ORR

"Kristin Espinasse is the pen friend we thought we had lost to email. She writes with sparkling insight as an American drawn by love to France, and it is a privilege to be let in to her daily life ... Her words have the freshness of a Provençal spring and her metaphors are as picturesque as her photographs of rural France. Her exquisitely crafted prose is a delight to read and her descriptions of everyday family life and the expatriate travails of fitting in are humorous and revealing of human nature. Yet I have come across the occasional thought or phrase so poignant and delicate that I have had to stop reading to blink, and so will you. Her blog format of using a French word or idiom from which to hang a portrait, a landscape or a vignette in words (no less works of art) tells us so much about France, the language and culture, the wines and cuisine, the people and the countryside. This is at once a Francophile's indulgence, a travelogue, a photo-journal, an occasional diary and a learn-French blog. It is also the 'happily ever after' of a love story and who can resist that?"

SUSHIL DAWKA

"Author Kristin Espinasse is a *trésor d'or*. Through her blog, she sends me a beautiful gift three times a week, which allows me, just for a few minutes, to return to my beloved France. And as a *petit bonus*, she helps this old *professeur* as she manages nearly every time to find some word or expression that is either new to me or long-forgotten.

Kristin not only shares her world with us—a world where languages and cultures intersect—but she opens her very life to us. As she invites us in, she allows the readers to become part of what she and husband Jean-Marc have created. Her skillful writing, combined with the wonder and magic of the South of France, has created a virtual family of loyal readers who eagerly wait for each new installment."

MICHAEL WRENN, French teacher

Blossoming
— IN —
Provence

KRISTIN ESPINASSE
author of "Words in a French Life"

FWD

Provence · France

*To my darling mom, Jules, who has helped me
to see the value in everyman,
and to look for the soft, often suffering,
heart in every person, no matter how rough…
no matter how refined.*

Table of Contents

Acknowledgments

I WOULD LIKE TO THANK FRENCH WORD-A-DAY READERS, WHO CONTINUE to encourage me to write and to photograph these episodes in a French life. *Mille mercies* for checking in "thrice-weekly" and for sticking with me no matter what the *topic du jour*.

Special thanks go to reader William C. Myers who volunteered, some time ago, to edit my missives—just as soon as they arrived in his inbox! It didn't matter that the corrections were submitted post-publication…the stories would one day reflect the changes, as they have here.

Remerciements to George E. Christian, Jr. and to Richard L. Christian, who began the long and tiresome job of correcting my split infinitives. They still check in, from time to time, to see if I am "keeping it together".

I thank my dear mom, Jules, for lending her ear during this "train ride" as she called it: the 21-Day Publishing Challenge that carried this project briskly forward to the finish line! Thanks for listening to my laughter and for hearing my tears. Your enthusiasm, ideas, and creative spirit have graced this book.

Tamara Dever and Erin Stark, with TLC Graphics, did a beautiful job on the cover and the interior of this edition. Their support took a great weight off my shoulders!

Thanks go out to Bruce T. Paddock for the extra grammar and review help. It was a relief knowing such help was only an e-mail away.

Finally I would like to thank those readers who helped me to edit this book by sending in corrections. (Forgive me if your name is not mentioned here; it wasn't easy to get everyone to step forward to receive due credit for their work; for those editors who wish to remain anonymous—or who missed the "Acknowledgments" call—please know that I am deeply grateful for the time you spent helping me to edit these stories!)

Many thanks again to…

Alyssa Ross Eppich, Betty Gleason, Michelle Taylor,
Sushil Dawka, Linda Louw, Cyndy Witzke, Bill Geery,
Diane Scott, Charles Orr, Della M. Seaton, Marcia Douglas,
Maureen C. Walsh, Priscilla Fleming Vayda, Jules Greer,
Stacy Lund, Heidi Ingham Stiteler, Mary Hunt Webb,
Avril Rustage-Johnston, Julia Willard, Tonya W. McNair,
Nancy Zuercher, Rina Rao, Olga Brown, Bruce T. Paddock,
Carrie Groves, Julianna Palazzolo, Christine Webb-Curtis,
Alison Johnston, Tim Averill, Janet Schilling Mowery,
Jan Leishman, Dawn Bouchard, Karen Cafarella,
Edie Schmidt, Carolyn Wade, Buffy Schilling,
Linda Williams Rorem, Sharon Howard Marchisello,
Leslie Duffy, Bettye Dew, Rob Tonkinson, Nigel Doyle,
Sandra E Chubb, Faye Stampe, Nick Keegan,
Judi Boeye Miller, Ian Pitt, Jackie Smith, Cheryl Anderson

Envíe

(ahn-vee)
noun, feminine

longing

I WAS STARING AT THE EMPTY BRANCHES OF OUR DOGWOOD TREE, willing its wooden limbs to quiver and send forth so many rosy blossoms, when I recognized a vague longing coming from within.

I stood up and walked over to the north window, threw open the painted green shutters and saw a small feathered creature pacing back and forth over a bed of crumbling leaves, just above the would-be strawberry patch.

I recognized another restless soul throwing its own will around, this one willing so many worms to pop out of the cold ground!

I looked at my dogwood, the red robin at its frozen patch, neither of us able to get the universe to dance for us.

On days like this the worms rejoice and the dogwoods, still as they are, cause willing hearts to stir.

It is hope that keeps us going.

Espoír

(es-pwar)
noun, masculine

hope

THE FOLLOWING LETTER IS AN INTIMATE LOOK INTO _LA NAISSANCE_ OF A CERtain "thrice-weekly" journal from France. This online blog began in October of 2002 following its earlier pen-and-paper beginnings—as letters that were sent via snail mail to a group of beta readers: my family and friends! For this opening story-letter, I have chosen a Wild West theme, one that seems fitting, considering my southwestern roots. Though I left the Phoenix desert half a life ago, a part of my heart forgot to board that plane to France.

To You, the Reader (A Story about You and Me)

In October of _deux mille deux_ I began a website, a _vitrine_ of sorts, for my writing. I put up a few published stories, a bio and _un livre d'or_, and waited beside my virtual mailbox, ginger ale in hand.

A few tumbleweeds blew past, but no publishers. My address, my website—_my writing_—remained in a cyber ghost town.

I continued to peddle my words, sending out queries for my stories. I did not sell many.

I thought to offer something to attract editors and publishers, and so I stepped out of my cyber-office and nailed up a sign. It read: "French Word-A-Day." I waited patiently for a customer. More tumbleweeds blew past. No publishers.

I continued to show up at the page, or keyboard, each morning and the stories collected like so many stars over a sleeping desert on a warm summer's night. As for *l'espoir*, I had that. Still, no publishers came.

But you did.

You must've seen the sign out front. You signed up for French words and accidentally found yourself in my French life. You must have said, "*Pourquoi pas?*" then pulled up a barstool, ordered a ginger ale, and settled in.

Your presence reassured me. I wrote and wrote and wrote a little more. And mostly I hoped you would not leave town when the next cyber stagecoach passed through. At least not until I figured out what it was I had to say.

Then one day you said: "Thank you for your missives," and I ran to my dictionary to look up that word. You also wrote: "Thank you for your vignettes."

"'Vignettes'! 'Vignettes'!" I giggled, doing a little square dance. I never knew what to call "it" besides an "essay" (which, I felt, was a spiffier term than "diary entry").

Many good months passed with small writing victories, and a former ghost town came to life.

But my *joie* was short-lived. A menace and a few mean-spirited e-mails arrived. I almost yearned for those tumbleweeds. Instead, I mentioned my *soucis* in a letter, and suddenly it was Showdown at the French Word-A-Day Corral! You showed up with your posse and told the bandits to get out of town. Then you turned to me and said: "Don't let the !@#& get you down!"

While others don't understand the life of a former desert rat-turned-French housewife-turned-*maman* and, recently, struggling *écrivaine* —you do.

At a shop in Draguignan, the *vendeuse* says: "Your name sounds familiar. What does your *husband* do?" I fall back into a slump, reminded that what I really am is a *pantoufle*-footed housewife with a backup of three loads of laundry and a sink full of dirty, mismatched *assiettes*.

I return home to the dirty dishes and the laundry—and to a letter from a reader, which says: "Thank you for your stories." I sit up straight, dust off my keyboard and am reminded that what I really am is a working writer—if only I will show up at the page, and write, each day.

So, thank you, dear Reader, for helping me to live my dream: for reading my—missives—and for your thoughtful words of support. Although publishers and agents may not be beating down my *porte*, each time I crack open the door—*there you are*.

In the new year, I'd like to continue with the stories, expanding the gist of this French Life. I hope you'll stay in town because I have figured out that I do, indeed, have something more to say. In fact, there is so much that I have not yet told you.

And while you know of the light-hearted, bubbly side of this expatriation, Real Life continues to rumble within my writing veins, like a rowdy, drunken saloon girl, wanting to be heard. Only I will need to slap her cheek, pour a bit of cool water over her head, take a tissue to her running mascara and tell her to *have faith*, that her story will be told, if she will only show up at the page.

May you, too, live your dream in the coming year.

Bien amicalement,

Kristin

———— French Vocabulary ————

la naissance
birth

deux mille deux
two thousand two

la vitrine
showcase

le livre d'or
guestbook

l'espoir
hope

pourquoi pas?
why not?

la joie
joy

un souci
worry

une maman
mom

un(e) écrivain(e)
writer

la vendeuse
saleslady

la pantoufle
(house) slipper

une assiette
plate

la porte
door

bien amicalement
best wishes, yours

Dédommagement

(day-doh-mazh-mahn)
noun, masculine

compensation

IN A MENSWEAR BOUTIQUE IN DRAGUIGNAN, I STAND AT THE COMPTOIR, hesitating between the powder-blue _chemise_ and the olive-green one. As I hem and haw, Jackie taps her foot, says either shirt will look good on Papa, and sighs for the _nième_ time. I remind her that if she is patient, I will buy her the mood ring she has been asking for—the one all her friends are sporting at school.

Next, the little bells hanging from the shop's entrance begin to jingle as the door opens and a small woman is swept in with the wind.

"_Bonjour, Messieurs Dames!_" she says, shivering from the cold mistral. The little woman has a purse hanging from the fold of her left arm and she is holding a small _boîte_ in her right hand. Her white hair falls just below her shoulders and is held back with an intricate tortoiseshell comb. She is wearing a dress, nylons, and little heels, which is more effort than a lot of women living this far north of the _Côte d'Azur_ put into suiting up in wintertime.

"Tell Hervé it is from Madame Kakapigeon!" the woman with the box and the heels says.

I look down to the blur of blue and green shirts and mutter the name I have just overheard, not sure I have heard correctly. "Kakapigeon"? Its sound causes me to blush. Poor thing, to have to go through life with such a name!

"*Tenez.*" Madame holds out the box, offering it to the saleswoman. "I'm off to the bank now! *Je n'ai plus un radis!*"

Our heads bob back and forth as my daughter and I witness the quirky exchange between the lively, gift-toting grandma and the store clerk. My eyes return to the *vendeuse*, who has taken the box of chocolates with its pretty cloth ribbon.

"*Au revoir, mes chéries,*" says the woman without a radish and, with that, the door swings shut making the jingle bells do their thing.

"What did she say her name was?" I ask, indiscreetly.

The saleslady smiles. "She calls herself 'Madame Caca Pigeon' because she is always feeding the pigeons from her balcony, just above our *magasin*. The well-fed birds are always 'messing' out in front of the boutique. Madame is sorry for the *salissure*, but it doesn't stop her from feeding her feathered friends. So every year, about this time, she comes in with her box of chocolates... *compliments of 'Madame Caca Pigeon'.*"

French Vocabulary

le comptoir
counter

la chemise
shirt

nième or énième
nth, umpteenth (time)

la vendeuse
saleslady

bonjour, Messieurs Dames
hello, everyone

une boîte
box

la Côte d'Azur
"The Blue Coast", The French Riviera

tenez (the verb is "tenir")
here, take it

ne pas/ne plus avoir un radis
to not/no longer have a cent
(or a penny) to one's name

au revoir, mes chéries
goodbye, my dears

le magasin
shop

la salissure
filth

Sapin

(sah-pahn)

noun, masculine

fir tree

WHEN MAX CAME INTO THE KITCHEN ANNOUNCING, "PAPA A ACHETÉ UN *sapin*," I folded the dishtowel, set it down and took a deep breath. I knew the Christmas tree would be trunk-size—all the better to fit into the back of an economy car—and not tall, like the spruce my mom used to whisk home (space limits were not an issue...Mom had the tree tied to the top of her '68 Camaro).

"*Cela suffira*," I reminded myself, hoping to have finally learned a lesson. *The tree, whatever it is, will be just what we need, and failing that, it will at least be real!* Only, when I saw what my husband, The Non-consumer, brought home this time, every nerve in my body became a live wire.

There in the center of the *salon* stood the most abominable tree that I had ever laid eyes on. I knew better than to open my mouth lest the dregs of language, French or English, should spew forth. Meanwhile my nerves began to short-circuit, and it was only a matter of time before the sparks reached my tongue, causing it to ignite.

"How much did you pay for it?" I questioned, teeth clamped.

"Twelve euros," Jean-Marc answered, jaws relaxed.

Twelve euros! That's 15 dollars...about how much he would spend on a decent bottle of wine—one that we might share in a single night. But a Christmas tree—that's something we could have spent a little more on, for we would enjoy it for an entire month!

After a moment of silence so thick you could hang tinsel on it, Jean-Marc challenged me: "You can take it back if you don't like it." His remark was delivered with the coolness of a peppermint candy cane.

"It is not for *me* to take back. YOU take it back!"

My husband's next response was to slam the door. I watched the ripple effect as the tinsel fell to the floor.

I looked down at the artificial *arbre*. *A Christmas tree should be at least as tall as a child,* I reasoned. Staring at the *sapin de Noël,* I noticed its mangled branches and its missing foliage. It was a fake fir, *one so cheap that it came with its own styrofoam ornaments!* And was that "presto tinsel" stuck to the branches?

I thought about the nine-foot-tall Colorado spruce that was Mom's joy to decorate. The ornaments were not automatically glued to the branches. *They were handmade!* One year Mom covered the tree with white *colombes* and pheasant *plumes.* She took the ordinary blue *boules* and dressed them up with peacock feathers (using only the fancy tops, or what she called the "eyes" of the feathers). Her zeal for holiday decorating didn't stop at the giant tree—she had those doves "flying" from the branches to the front door!

My eyes returned to the bedroom door, which had just been slammed shut. I looked back down at the Christmas tree. The longer I stared, the uglier it appeared.

"It is the ugliest tree that I have ever seen!" I declared, and pulled off what decorations Jean-Marc and Jackie had put up. I yanked apart the tree and shoved it into the stupid bag from which it came. Still smarting, I returned to the kitchen and slammed the dirty pots

and pans around in the sink, *the sink without a garbage disposal!* Only in France!

"You're so complicated," my Frenchman used to say as I struggled to adapt to his country, to his ways, to his small-treed holidays. Over the years, I began to suspect that he had a point. Indignation turned to industry as, little by little, I began ousting the surplus and the *super-flu*—learning the difference between want and *besoin*, all the while simplifying, *simplifying!*

The sum of all that effort now stood before me, concrete in form, via this, the simplest tree.

"But I want a COMPLICATED Christmas treeeeeee!" I cried out, shoving the sponge back into the pan as I scoured and glowered. "I want a showy, superfluous, SUPERCALIFRAGILISTIC spruce!"

Just then I heard the rustle of faux branches and a whisper....

"*Il est beau!*" Max was saying to his sister.

"*Oui, regarde,*" she agreed, softly.

I listened to the clanking of aluminum bulbs....Peeking around the corner, I witnessed the scene. Max had pulled the tree back out of the bag and reassembled it. The branches, still *tordues*, now had a colorful array of bulbs, some chipped, some dusty, some new—all carefully hung. There were so many decorations that the empty parts, where branches seemed to be missing, were now filled in.

Jean-Marc was on his knees searching for an electrical outlet. Finding one, he plugged in the tree lights, but when he turned to reach for the switch...my hand was already on it. Our eyes locked.

My husband smiled as I flipped the switch. When the tree lights went on, the room came to a swift hush. In the silence she appeared: *La Joie*—an *étincelle* here, a sparkle there—happiness filling the room, its presence so real, so palpable, you could hang tinsel on it.

French Vocabulary

Papa a acheté un sapin
Papa's bought a Christmas tree

çela suffira
that'll suffice

le salon
living room

un arbre
tree

le sapin de Noël
Christmas tree

la colombe
dove

la plume
feather

la boule
ball

le superflu
superfluity

le besoin
need

il est beau
it is beautiful (tree)

oui, regarde
yes, look

tordu(e)
twisted, bent

la joie
joy

une étincelle
spark, sparkle

Pêle-Mêle

(pel-mel)

higgledy-piggledy, any old how

JEAN-MARC PULLED INTO THE SNOW-N-SLUSH PARKING LOT BEHIND L'EQUIPE Hotel, got out and searched for the entrance. Ignoring the two-foot-tall board marked ENTREE, he side-trekked around the back of the building. I think he purposely misses these "how-to" signs and, in so doing, he turns life into one man's perpetual back-to-nature quest (and French boot camp for his prissy American bride).

Max, Jackie and Miss Priss followed, dragging our bags up the steel-grated stairs reserved for employees; we hiked around the brasserie to find ourselves back on track with the *normal* guests who approached the hotel in a conventional fashion.

Three hours earlier, just before heading out for the French Alps, I'd talked my style-unconscious husband out of his Glad Bag valise so that this time we were not stealing past other hotel guests—me with a duct-taped suitcase, the kids with a plastic laundry basket "drawer-for-the-weekend" and my husband with two hefty garbage bags (the deluxe kind with built-in handles, and not the cheap ones with the detachable plastic yellow string), contents thrown in *pêle-mêle*.

In the hotel lobby, we were greeted by three French mutts—which explained the surprise-on-ice we'd sidestepped out on the Path Less Traveled. The dogs' owner stubbed out her cigarette before checking the reservations book.

"*Chambres* 15 and 16," she said, pulling two keys from a wallboard of 23 hooks.

Max pointed to the keychain and quizzed his sister: Did she know what the small, abstract wooden carving represented?

"*Un castor!*" she correctly guessed.

We climbed four levels of *moquette*-covered stairs, pausing to catch our breath in front of a needlepoint wall hanging, its thick yarn...in mustard, orange and black...looped loosely across a cotton canvas. Plastic flowers, now faded, punctuated each landing.

Two floors up, Jean-Marc pushed the long metal key into the keyhole at room 15. He had to tug the door forward as he turned the key to the right and to the left (this tugging and key jiggling was in response to an *indice* he was discovering in real time—as he watched a demonstration given by the young woman standing next to a vacuum cleaner and cart two doors down.

No framed needlepoint art in the rooms, just more plastic flowers and more synthetic-carpet tile. Each side of the bed in room 15 had candle lighting—except a plastic flame stood in for a fiery one. Behind a vinyl accordion door, the bathroom, which included a plastic flamingo pink shower head draped over decades old *robinetterie*, smelled like a porta-potty.

"No, it doesn't smell like that," Jean-Marc retorted. "It smells like a hospital."

"Oh," I said, encouraged. The kids' room was a repeat of our own, except that it had twin beds.

The stringy sound of a violoncello filtered in from *chambre* 14, the cellist's glorious musical notes almost canceling out the infant's

cries from the room above; such wailing from deep in the icy French woods, along with the bow and string (*sans* arrow) next door, seemed in keeping with one Frenchman's return to the Land Before Time, and the hotel decor, though not prehistoric, had that barbaric feel with just the right dose of vulgar to temper Miss Priss's great expectations.

I watched my husband unpack his bags with gusto, and it occurred to me to face our circumstances with a similar verve or *joie de vivre*.

With a little effort, I could begin to see our surroundings in a new light: no longer did the room feel oppressive. With renewed thinking, I began to feel a flutter inside my spirit, as a new sense of adventure was born. One that would sustain me, again and again, each time my husband reserved a hotel room....

French Vocabulary

l'entrée (f)
entrance

pêle-mêle
in confused haste

la chambre
room

le castor
beaver

la moquette
carpet

un indice
clue

la robinetterie
plumbing

sans
without

la joie de vivre
joy of living

Petite Amie

(peuh-teet-ah-me)
noun, feminine

girlfriend

On Friday, the *lendemain* of Jean-Marc's fortieth birthday, a florist's van pulled up to our front gate. I watched as the driver handed over a lipstick-red ceramic vase with a single orchid inside. Halfway up the exotic flower a hummingbird clung, its delicate wings poised for flight.

When I noticed Jean-Marc smiling as big as *Le Chat de Cheshire*, I ran out to meet him, curious to know who was sending him flowers. It had to be a female. Probably my sister Heidi, I reasoned. Who else could it be?

"*C'est qui cette garce?*" "Who's the tart that sent you the flowers?" I teased, with mock *jalousie*, not at all referring to my sister but to an imaginary rival. The birthday boy took his time reaching into the vase to retrieve the gift card.

"Aha...!" he exclaimed, adding to the intrigue.

"Who is it from?" I insisted. The quiver in my voice belied the confident smile on my face.

When Jean-Marc named his former *petite amie*, my face turned as white as the dress I wore at my wedding. The same dress that the Other Woman had once sat scrutinizing.

The Other Woman is she who appeared on the scene when I came home to America having just met Jean-Marc. (We'll call her "Owch" for the Other Woman [after I] Came Home). *Owch* and Jean-Marc dated, broke up, and dated again before breaking up for good. Sure of his decision, Jean-Marc invited me back into his life, also "for good" (I hoped).

On the morning of my wedding day Owch called her Ex (my Future) for directions to the church, and, in so doing, managed to pee on my parade. (*I hope that the reader will excuse any verbal crass-ness and instead conjure up an image of one woman's (Owch's) attempt to both mark her former territory and cloud up an otherwise bright day*). And so my wedding day began with Owch and, as you will soon see, ended with Owch for a double wedding whammy. Indeed, Owch was a thorn in my very swollen side.

Owch, with the shiny black bob, did not show up this time in painted-on-the-body black leather, but wore two dresses on my wed-ding day: one to the church and another shorter, plungier, blacker number to the wedding feast. Big as I was (or felt), I didn't have another "little number" to change into, as Owch did. What with my growing girth... it wasn't an option. And so I stood, not in a fitted dress like my rival's, but just fitting into my gown with its fat cloth buttons riding down my back like marshmallows. And though I should have been thanking my lucky stars that the wedding dress fit at "five weeks," I could only think of how frumpy I looked compared to Mademoiselle Owch, the Parisian panther.

At around two in the morning, I found myself face-to-face with Owch, in her clingy dress and concave stomach. We were seated at a table next to the dance floor, where Owch had spent the evening shaking it up, uP, UP! With the rise of her skirt I noticed her legs, which were taut, tanned and untamed by nylons as she crossed them on the chair before me. My own legs were covered in opaque white

stockings and hidden beneath some increasingly constrictive *crêpe de chine*.

Owch took another drag from her slim cigarette before aiming dead center between my eyes, which crossed in disbelief as I followed the train of smoke that escaped from her pursed lips. A thick ashen wall of defense now separated us. From the opposite side of the front line, the enemy spoke.

"So, when is the baby due?"

I was too stunned to answer. My eyes dropped to the floor, but not before catching on Owch's blood-red nails, which curled like claws around a glass of champagne.

FAST FORWARD NOW... MY OWN FINGERNAILS, TRIMMED SHORT AND UNPOL-ished, crowned insistent fingers that snapped the gift card out of my husband's hand. I studied the fake hummingbird that accompanied the flower. I felt an urge to swat the delicate creature as one would a fly.

Before I could learn the true answer, Jean-Marc assured me: "I was only kidding you!" Reading the card, I saw for myself that the flowers were not from Owch. *Ahhh....*

They were from someone else!

Do forgive me if I do not tell you just who sent the orchid. For, like a well-covered woman (whether in *crêpe de chine* or plain ol' cotton), it is the mystery that adds to the allure. And it is the allure that endures.

One last note, this time to my son: Max, your father and I were married in a civil ceremony—two months prior to the religious ceremony—in Marseilles's magical Bagatelle. You can put your calculator away now, Honey, and know that God was on our side, even if the French law sometimes wasn't. (I'll tell you about your mother's stint as an illegal alien when you are a little older. For now, do as I say and not as I do and remember your great-grandfather Gordon's words of wisdom: When you are around trouble, you are in it!)

French Vocabulary

le lendemain
the next day

Le chat (m) de Cheshire
The Cheshire Cat

la jalousie
jealousy

la petite amie (le petit ami)
girlfriend (boyfriend)

Bagatelle
the name of the town hall in
Marseilles's 8ème arrondissement

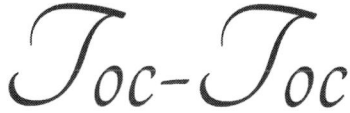Toc-Toc

(tok-tok)

knock knock

EVERYTHING ABOUT MARTINE COULD BE KNOWN BY HER KNOCK: UNHESI-tating, energetic, persistent. It was the kind of knock a policeman might use: "*Toc-toc-toc!* I know you're in there. Come out, come out!"

Though law-abiding, Martine was always on the run. "I passed by your house last night," she'd say, "on my way home from work. Your shutters were open so I closed them for you." I guessed she had figured out that my husband was away a lot on business and that I needed a reminder to lock up my windows for the night, as the villagers do.

When Martine wasn't watching over my home, she was filling it. She brought the children strawberries from the farmers' market and she brought me fresh cabbage—then stayed to stuff and bake it.

"It's good, isn't it?" she'd say, of the stuffed *chou*. "You love it! It is delicious!" While I ate, she would set about reorganizing my *frigo*. "All of the condiments and spreads go here!" she'd say, gathering the ketchup and the pickles and the *tapenade* from the back of the fridge and placing them in the door compartments.

If I complimented her on her dress, she would straighten her five-foot frame, hold her head high, and raise her hand with a flourish. "*Je suis belle, non?* Just look at me! *Bella!*"

Her teeth, one slightly and charmingly bent over the other in front, were always showing, because her mouth was always smiling. She was Italian with a dark complexion, her hair was bleached light, her makeup heavy, and her figure—which she decorated with pride—somewhere in between. Martine did not have hang-ups or low self-esteem; she had no time to question or to second-guess. Like her knock—*Toc-toc-toc*! Come out, come out!—she was direct.

"Get in the car!" she ordered, when personal doubts had begun to consume me. Struggling as a young mother, an *étrangère*, and a wife, I decided I had nothing to lose by allowing this colorful new friend to steer me out of my *tristesse*.

Martine drove, speeding across the countryside and over a narrow bridge—edging so close to the guardrail that I shrieked, "*Martine!*" When I had recovered from the fright, I turned to my friend:

"How do you know you're not going to hit that rail? How can you judge so well?"

"*Ce n'est rien*! You just need to take driving lessons, know the size of your car—*sois confiante*!"

True, I thought, forgetting about the guardrail and remembering my earlier self-doubts. It was high time, now, to step confidently into some of the new roles that I had been given since moving to France. Wife, mother, French resident...the ability to fully carry out these roles was there, somewhere, inside of me. I just needed to let go of that guardrail and have *confiance*!

When we had cleared the bridge, Martine abruptly pulled the car over and reached past me to the glove compartment, from which she produced a folded piece of paper.

"*Écoute bien*," she said. "I am going to read you something...."

(*Continued on page 34...*)

French Vocabulary

toc-toc-toc
knock-knock-knock

le chou
cabbage

le frigo
fridge

la tapenade
pureed olive spread

je suis belle, non?
I am beautiful, aren't I?

un étranger, une étrangère
foreigner

la tristesse
gloominess

ce n'est rien
it's nothing (it's easy)

sois confiant(e)
be confident

écoute bien
listen closely

la confiance
confidence

HERE IS THE POEM THAT MARTINE READ TO ME. (OR RATHER, SHE READ THE French translation, "*Tu seras un homme mon fils*," by André Maurois.)

"*If*——"

If you can keep your head when all about you
Are losing theirs and blaming it on you;
If you can trust yourself when all men doubt you,
But make allowance for their doubting too;

If you can wait and not be tired by waiting,
Or, being lied about, don't deal in lies,
Or, being hated, don't give way to hating,
And yet don't look too good, nor talk too wise;

If you can dream—and not make dreams your master;
If you can think—and not make thoughts your aim;
If you can meet with Triumph and Disaster

And treat those two imposters just the same;
If you can bear to hear the truth you've spoken
Twisted by knaves to make a trap for fools,
Or watch the things you gave your life to, broken,

And stoop and build 'em up with worn-out tools;
If you can make one heap of all your winnings
And risk it on one turn of pitch-and-toss,
And lose, and start again at your beginnings
And never breathe a word about your loss;

If you can force your heart and nerve and sinew
To serve your turn long after they are gone,
And so hold on when there is nothing in you

Except the Will which says to them: "Hold on!"
If you can talk with crowds and keep your virtue,
Or walk with kings—nor lose the common touch;
If neither foes nor loving friends can hurt you;
If all men count with you, but none too much;

If you can fill the unforgiving minute
With sixty seconds' worth of distance run,
Yours is the Earth and everything that's in it,
And—which is more—you'll be a Man, my son!

RUDYARD KIPLING

Épuiser

(ay-pwee-zay)

to exhaust, to wear out

Max has paired an orange-and-blue T-shirt with red sweat pants. I gaze at my son, thinking about how I need to explain to him the basics of fashion. For one, he needs to learn the rule on colors that clash: "No wearing orange with red!"

On second thought, forget about the color wheel! Precious few years remain in which I'll be able to witness daily this wake-up-and-dress-with-abandon innocence. Besides, my mission this morning is not to critique Max's wardrobe, but to find him a project.

Earlier, at the breakfast table, when I could no longer eat in peace after the kids began bouncing off the walls, I realized I might channel some of that energy...into home improvement!

"You know those baseball cards of yours?" I ask Max.

My son looks lost.

"I mean, the basketball *cartes*..."

"*Quoi?*"

"Oh...I'm talking about the *cartes de foot*—the ones you like to trade with your friends!"

"*Ah, oui...*"

"Well, if you sweep the back patio—really well—for, say, one-half hour and not five seconds—then I will buy you a pack of those cards. How much do they cost, by the way?"

"*Quarante centimes*," Max answers, grinning from ear to ear.

"O.K., that'll work!"

Max begins his chore with gusto, sweeping, swooping, and swiveling that brush-on-a-stick. Occasionally he stops to admire his reflection in the *porte-fenêtre*....

He turns the broom sideways...and heaves up the make-believe ten-ton barbell. When the champion weight lifter is satisfied with his world record, he returns the barbell/broom to its vertical position and resumes sweeping the patio.

Noticing him push the broom hard against the ground, making great exaggerated swoops, I intervene:

"Max, you are going to wear yourself out if you continue like that! Watch me," I suggest, taking the broom. Accomplishing a few feather-light sweeps across the patio, I begin to sing:

Il ne faut pas t'épuiser
Non, non, non, ne t'épuise pas...

I sing as only a mother can, before her child and no other, belting out the make-it-up-as-you-go tune.

Il faut pas t'épuiser
Non, non, non, ne t'épuise pas...

I stop the broom in its tracks, to experience a flashback of a similar scene. I am at my mom's cabin, near Saguaro Lake, back home in Arizona. I am pushing a three-ton broom around the living room.

"Here, give me that!" my mom says, stubbing out her cigarette. She proceeds, light on her feet, to sweep the hardwood floor of her *salon*. She is in full make-up, though we are an hour's drive from civilization, and her hair is gathered into a French twist and secured by a battalion of bobby pins. She is wearing cowboy boots, the ones with the spurs. Instead of singing, she's humming. "Don't struggle so," is her message. "Lighten up and the job will be easier."

"Watch this," she says, sailing across the room, with the broom in her hands. In the background, televangelist Freddy Price is spreading the Word, causing us to pause now and again to shout "Amen!"

Mom's got that broom and she is fluttering across the wood floor, with the lightness of a butterfly.

"I used to sweep like you," she says, "until I learned to sweep like this!" As I watch her, an overwhelming urge is building in me to sweep! I want that broom just as I want to try on a new pair of roller skates. My mom hands me the broom and returns to her desk to paint her nails copper. Behind her, there is a wall of books. I recognize the hardbound editions; I can still see them perfectly in my mind, just as they were placed on the bookshelves of my childhood.

There were, among others, *Atlas Shrugged* by Ayn Rand, James Michener's *The Source*, and *My Mother/Myself* by Nancy Friday. And there was Mom's treasure: William Gurnall's *The Christian in Complete Armour*, the epic masterpiece written between 1655-1662. She had the giant red leather three-volume set.

Her library aside...the image of my mom sweeping returns to me whenever I find myself making a brick wall out of any hard-to-begin activity, whether it be writing or washing floors or rearing children. The more I push, the more I struggle, the more I wear myself out and despair.

I hand the broom back to Max and return to the breakfast table to observe him from the window. He pushes the broom, stopping to pass it between his legs, then sweeps, sweeps, sweeps, to stop again and make another pass. Only a kid could make a basketball out of a *balai*. Only a mother-in-spurs could tame a two-ton broom into becoming a butterfly.

As for me, I'll quit building brick walls today and remember to flutter instead of fluster, to pass or dribble instead of pound and tremble, to lighten up like the *papillons* that fly across the soon-to-bloom poppy fields outside my door.

Il faut pas t'épuiser
Non, non, non, ne t'épuise pas...

French Vocabulary

le petit déjeuner
breakfast

la carte
card

les cartes de foot
soccer (trading) cards

quoi?
what?

ah, oui
oh, yes

quarante centimes
forty French cents

la porte-fenêtre
French door

il ne faut pas t'épuiser
you mustn't wear yourself out, no...don't wear yourself out

le salon
living room

le balai
broom

le papillon
butterfly

Tapenade

(tapenahd)
noun, feminine

pureed olive spread

WHEN MY MOTHER-IN-LAW, MICHÈLE-FRANCE, LOOKS OUT THE WINDOW of her two-room apartment, she can just about see the *paquebots* leaving Marseilles's Old Port, for Casablanca. That is when the memories of childhood in her beloved *Maroc* come flowing back.

One floor below, Janine is also staring out to sea from behind her tiny kitchen table, where she sits with her crippled little dog and waits for the telephone to ring.

At times like these, when nostalgia and solitude weigh on their hearts, Michèle-France's 4th floor apartment turns into a spicy olive-paste factory as my mother-in-law puts her *petite voisine* to work; her neighbor's job is to remove the *noyaux* from the olives.

Great bowls of hollow black fruit are soon delivered by 3rd Floor Janine up to 4th Floor Michèle-France, who mixes the olives with a couple of bay leaves, some anchovies, capers...and a few top-secret ingredients. The mixture is then marinated overnight. The next morning the *mélange* is poured into a food processor for grinding.

All that pitting and pulverizing plucks the loneliness right out of the women's souls, and the resulting *pots de tapenade* have the women

on the train in no time, delivering the latest batch of *bonheur* to family and friends.

On Wednesday, Michèle-France brought over six mustard jars full of *tapenade*—three flavored with fresh basil leaf, three with red bell pepper—for Max's birthday celebration. As we sat at the table chatting, I spread spoonfuls of the dark olive paste over a sliced baguette before sinking my teeth in...*Crunch!*

"Janine doesn't always get the pits out of the olives," Michèle-France confided. "She can't see that well. I always know when she's left a *noyau* behind because my mixer goes *CRACK CRACK!*"

"*Je vois...*" I sympathized with my *belle-mère* as we held our sore jaws in our hands while our own teeth went *crack-crack* over yet another missed pit. But that didn't stop us from savoring the latest *bocal de bonheur*, and raising a toast to *la petite voisine* Janine.

French Vocabulary

le paquebot
liner, steamship

le Maroc
Morocco

la petite voisine, le petit voisin
term of endearment for "little neighbor"

le pot
jar

le mélange
mixture

la tapenade
olive paste made from crushed olives, capers,
anchovies, garlic, lemon juice and olive oil

le bonheur
happiness

le noyau
pit

je vois
I see

la belle-mère
mother-in-law

le bocal de bonheur
jar of happiness

Lance

(lahnse)
noun, feminine

a spear

WHILE PREPARING FOR A ROMANTIC GETAWAY, I ASKED MY HUSBAND WHERE he had set his suitcase. That was when he informed me he wasn't taking one. I guessed the shirt on his back would be, once again, sufficient for an overnight trip, and that he would just borrow my toothbrush and deodorant, *comme d'habitude*.

No matter how many times I object—*Beurk!*—regarding the toothbrush-sharing and—*C'est pour les femmes!*—concerning the deodorant, he does as he pleases. Such accoutrements and hygienic hassles are unimportant details—downright snags—in his very down-to-earth existence.

Meantime, life beckons with its rugged, cobalt-blue sea and its remote, Mediterranean coves now bursting with succulent sea urchins. Such were the treasures we were about to rediscover over the weekend, on the quaint French island of Porquerolles, where Jean-Marc had reserved a Valentine's Day retreat.

On the eve of our departure, I found my husband in the kitchen fashioning an impromptu spear from a floor mop.

"Where'd you get that?" I questioned, pointing to my mop.

"I didn't think you used it," he said, innocently.

"That's beside the point!"

Rather than argue, Jean-Marc began to pierce holes in one end of the mop, having already removed its stringy top....

"Hey! What are you doing?!" I asked as I stood there, goggle-eyed, not sure whether I really cared about the mop, but shocked, all the same, to witness its demise.

Jean-Marc opened the silverware drawer and reached for *une fourchette*. He had found an old shoelace and was now using it to tie the fork to the end of the mop. For an instant, I was tempted to calculate just how many gasoline points we had saved to pay for that fork...only this, too, was beside the point. Come to think of it, just what was the point? What on earth was he rigging together this time? A hunting *lance*, I think he said it was?

"*Laisse tomber!*" I thought to myself, for the umpteenth time in 10 years of marriage. I walked out of the kitchen, leaving my husband to explore his creative side—at the expense of yet another cooking or cleaning utensil.

By the time we arrived in the coastal town of Hyères to catch the *navette*, I'd long since gotten over the novelty of the wacky, home-made hunting implement. It was when we began to receive odd looks from the other passengers that I realized just how goofy (worse—psychopathic!) my husband appeared, sitting there with a blank look on his face and the mop-fork spear at his side. One woman got up and changed seats. Another pulled her child close. A few people whispered. More than one set of eyes narrowed.

Jean-Marc sat oblivious to the commotion. I'm certain he was dreaming of the day's catch—all those spiky *oursins* (and the delicacy inside them: sea urchin roe), the ones he would soon rake in with his clever, multi-purpose *outil*.

There he sat, dreaming of the new frontiers he would be forging with the aid of his...mop. He was terribly impressed by how the mop-spear doubled as a walking stick.

"Look," he said, tap-tap-tapping it against the ground, stepping gleefully forward and backward for effect.

I shook my head, reminded of life's simple pleasures, and of my husband, who is like the child who pushes aside the newly-acquired toy to play with the champagne cork. May he continue to free himself of life's superficial snags, to enjoy the ongoing adventure that thunders beneath his French feet. May he go forward, unadorned by all that is *superflu*. May fashion or deodorant never hinder him from his burning quest to discover the rugged coastline, where shellfish rock gently beneath the shimmering sea.

Should the road less traveled ever get too bumpy, he'll have his mopstick to lean on—and he'll have me, too.

French Vocabulary

comme d'habitude
as usual

beurk!
ew ! yuck!

c'est pour les femmes
it's for women

une fourchette
fork

une lance
spear

laisse tomber! (laisser tomber)
let it go! forget about it!

la navette
shuttle (ferry boat)

un oursin
a sea urchin

un outil
a tool

le superflu
excess

Noeud

(neuh)
noun, masculine

bow

HEADING DOWN THE *COULOIR*, I HEAR A LOW HUM COMING FROM MY daughter's room. Peering around the door, I find Jackie sitting on the floor, one leg extended, the other bent with the knee up. Her arms encircle the bent leg with its scraped *genou* and her fingers are caught in her shoelaces. With a sigh, she frees her hands from the tangle, only to pick up the laces again before repeating this mantra:

> *Pour faire un noeud*
> *Je fais une boucle*
> *Je tourne autour*
> *Je passe par le petit trou*
> *et je tire...Raté!*

> To make a bow
> I fashion a loop
> I circle around it
> I pass through the little hole
> and pull...Missed!

Jackie brushes a lock of hair away from her face and begins again. As my eight-year-old repeats the chant, I can just imagine the pressure she must be under. Earlier, her brother had warned her that if she couldn't tie her shoes by the time she was twelve, she would be *la honte* of middle school.

I think about my disservice to my daughter in opting for all those Mary Janes and tennis shoes with the Velcro closures. What was a helpful shortcut for a busy mother is now an *honteux* obstacle for her daughter.

Hands now clasped in supplication, I stand quietly by the door listening to a few more shoelace-tying attempts:

Pour faire un noeud... To make a bow...

I watch, front teeth pressing into lower lip, until the last line of the mantra changes:

...et voilà!
...and there I have it!

With a sigh of relief, I slip away unnoticed and carry on down the hall, my heart swelling. That's my girl!

French Vocabulary

le couloir
hallway, corridor

le genou
knee

la honte
disgrace, shame

honteux (honteuse)
disgraceful

Guerre

(gair)
noun, feminine

war, warfare

At Cafe de la Tour I found a seat close to the *porte-fenêtre* for a nice view of the village square on market day. The *serveuse* cleared away the dirty ashtray and *les petites tasses* before I set down three baguettes, my purse and my keys, and nodded *bonjour* to the strangers on my left.

Jean-Claude, the former *patron* (his daughter Sophie now runs the place), was seated at the opposite table with two burly locals. The three retired men had their noses in a pile of black-and-white photos and that is when I noticed for the first time that Jean-Claude owned one, a nose, that is. *He had shaved off his legendary mustache!*

Gone was the dramatic white *flip* which swooped up and out at either end. The once soft, uniform curl was like a giant eyelash that batted as he spoke. So long was that mustache that it curled right up over the tip of his nose *and covered it.*

"What? You didn't know?" Jean-Claude turned to greet me. He then filled me in on the little accident he had had along the *Promenade des Anglais* in Nice, where he had had an inspiration while watching the young freestylers. That is when the idea struck him *to*

*borrow one of the boys' BMX bikes...*only to quickly discover that he, Jean-Claude, had a fear of heights!

Dangling over the edge of a mini ramp, Jean-Claude's fall was imminent, and he landed smack on his shiny head. Thirty some odd stitches later, he still hasn't lost that radiant smile—although he did lose all of his front teeth—which explains the "bald spot" above his upper lip, one that now matches the smoothness of his head, the mustache having been shaved off when the dental work began.

"That must have been traumatizing!" I said of the well-known mustache, thinking about the loss of what could surely be considered a limb. Jean-Claude looked at me blankly before that beaming smile returned.

"*Ce n'était rien,*" It was nothing, he said thoughtfully, his eyes returning to the pile of old war photos.

Changing the subject, Jean-Claude handed me the black-and-white images, explaining that the photos were of the *Libération*, taken when American soldiers arrived in Les Arcs-sur-Argens, freeing the village from German occupation. I recognized our town's square; only, instead of the realtor's office there was a little boutique with a wooden sign that read "*Mode.*"

The men seated beside Jean-Claude were now recounting war stories. As Jean-Claude and I studied the photos, I heard bits and pieces of the burly men's conversation: "*...the parachutists landed...the maquisards fought...a soldier fell right out front...*"

"Look at the hats!" Jean-Claude cried out, loud enough to muffle the voices next to him. He began pointing to a photo in which a crowd of men stood in the village square, their heads kept warm with those stylish newsboy caps. While J.-C. and I looked at '40s fashions, the men seated next to us continued commenting and I picked up scraps of their grim dialogue—

"...*the Americans captured the Germans...prisoner of war...chained to the soldier...*" but Jean-Claude's well-timed exclamations drowned out most of the sad and violent images.

"Look at the children! So many children!" Jean-Claude piped back in, this time pointing to a photo in which some little kids were seated on the church steps, but I found it hard to concentrate on the image. Instead, my ears were trying to tune in to the table beside us, where the men continued their remembrances:

"...*the prisoners were marched off...blood...*"

"Ah, *le platane* is still there! Do you recognize the old tree?" Jean-Claude enthused, but the men's bleak commentary continued: "...*American soldier shot down by the train station, died right there...the American and German were hit, killed by the same blow!...*"

"That's Pascal," Jean-Claude chimed in, his back now to the men seated at the table next to ours. I looked at the photo of a skinny, grimy-faced kid, shorts rolled up, socks falling down around his bony ankles.

"His family still owns the *carrosserie* down the street," he added, ignoring his tablemates. "Ah, *wonderful man*! He must've been six or seven years old in this photo." Jean-Claude shook his head, but there was a gentle smile on his face, that is, until I voiced a lingering question:

"Can you tell me about the war?" I asked, trusting Jean-Claude to paint a sensitive portrait of life here in Les Arcs-sur-Argens during WWII. Instead he threw me another one of those famous blank stares.

"*C'est intéressant...la guerre,*" I said, saying anything to fill in the silence.

"No, *war is not interesting!*" Jean-Claude said, swatting me several times over the shoulder with the photos, in mock condemnation.

"Look at that gun!" I said.

"Ah, the chewing *gum!*" Jean-Claude replied, cleverly evading the subject, and ignoring the photo that the men beside us had just handed over. "The Americans and their chewing gum! The soldiers, who were often called 'Joe', loved their chewing gum!" he said with that contagious smile.

I sipped my *café-au-lait* and watched Jean-Claude point out rosy details in the old, dark photos. He was seeing the children's smiles, the fashions, the beautiful trees, as well as hearing the whir of wheels riding up the seaside ramp and his own freestyle foray into...well, never mind the crash. On he went, painting his own postwar portrait of Provence and, though not erasing the past, he expertly drew blanks over the pain.

French Vocabulary

la porte-fenêtre
French window

la serveuse
barmaid

une petite tasse
an espresso coffee cup

le patron (la patronne)
business owner

la Libération
the freeing from foreign occupation

la mode
fashion

le maquisard
"man of the maquis" (wild Mediterranean scrubland)
or French resistance fighter hidden in the
forests and mountains during WWII

le platane
plane tree

la carrosserie
automobile body shop

Pétillant

(pay-tee-yahn)

sparkling, bubbly, fizzy

WHEN I FINISHED MOPPING THE APRICOT TILES OF OUR HOME, I CONSIDERED my next mission: to prevent so many little feet from pottering across the clean *carrelage*. The messy four o'clock *goûter* would just have to take place outside today! I would not risk cake crumbs or spilled drinks on this clean floor!

I gathered Max, his two neighborhood friends, and Jackie into a football huddle out on the patio.

"Listen closely. I don't want any of you coming in the house, *d'accord*? I've just cleaned the floor, and I have GUESTS coming soon."

The French boys turned to Max and Jackie for a translation:

"*Elle ne veut pas qu'on aille dans la maison car elle vient de nettoyer par terre et elle a des INVITÉS demain.*"

The kids gave serious nods of comprehension.

"Understand?" I checked.

"*Oui*," they confirmed.

Satisfied, I brought out individually wrapped chocolate sponge cakes, fruit and water, and placed a stack of plastic *gobelets* next to the snacks.

"Do you need anything else?" I inquired.

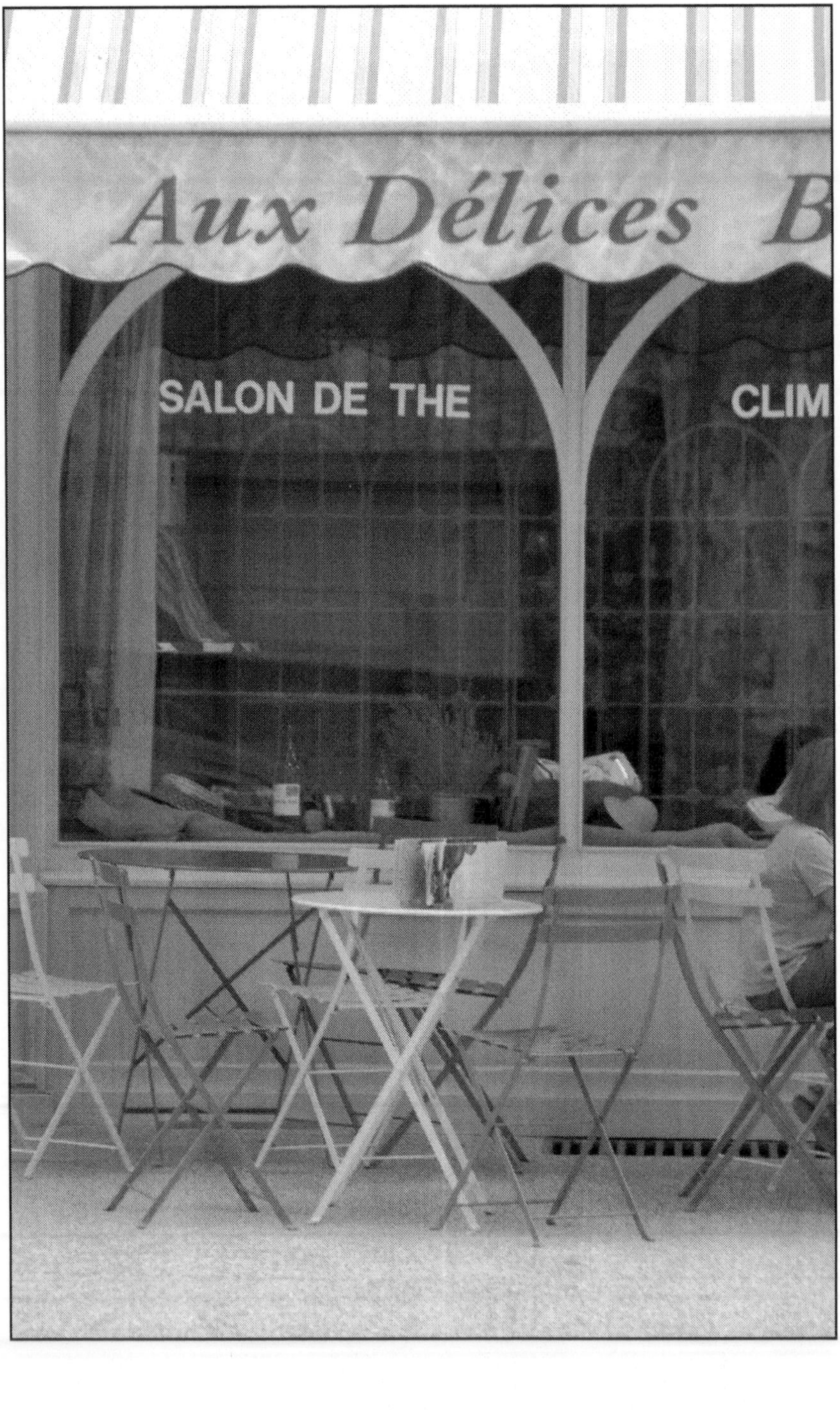
Aux Délices B
SALON DE THE
CLIM

"*Non.*"

"Sure?"

"*C'est bon, merci,*" they replied, politely.

"Okay, now remember, don't go into the house. Keep it clean for my guests!"

I left the kids and the cakes and went inside to tidy up another room. Ten minutes later I noticed a suspicious calm.... Running for the kitchen, I stumbled onto a trail of *sucre!*

I followed the crunchy path to its source, at which point my eyes shot out of their sockets on witnessing the sticky scene.

"What ARE you doing?" I questioned my children.

Jackie was holding a plastic cup *filled to the brim with just-picked mint leaves.* Max was standing beside her, pouring sugar from box to cup; some of the sweet crystals landed inside, but the rest of the sugar hit the rim of the cup and shot out across the floor!

"*L'eau à la menthe,*" Max explained, concentrating on his aim.

Astonished, I followed my son and my daughter outside to where the neighbor boys waited patiently, bottles of sparkling water in hand, ready to pour the *eau pétillante* into the cups of sugar and mint. Another trail, this time of mint leaves, began at the flower bed and ended beneath the boys' feet.

I observed the kids with the virgin mint juleps in their hands. I noticed how careful they were with their gestures as they raised their full glasses to their mouths for refreshment. They looked my way with smiles of gratitude.

And then it hit me. What I had failed to realize, back inside my spotless house, was that my guests had already arrived! My all-important *invités* had been here all along! Others twice their size might be on their way over but, meantime, here were some visitors with a thirst for life! How much more could a hostess ask for?

I quickly made my way back into the house—across the sticky floor... and over to the sticky freezer door—to get my important guests some more ice for their fancy drinks. It is never too late to be a caring and considerate *maîtresse de maison*.

French Vocabulary

le carrelage
tiled floor

le goûter
afterschool snack

d'accord
okay

**Elle ne veut pas qu'on aille dans la maison
car elle vient de nettoyer par terre
et elle a des INVITÉS demain**
She doesn't want us to go in the house because
she's washed the floor and has GUESTS tomorrow

le gobelet
cup

c'est bon, merci
it's good, thanks

le sucre
sugar

l'eau (f) à la menthe
water with mint

l'eau (f) pétillante
sparkling water

l'invité(e)
guest

la maîtresse de maison
the "mistress of the house" (hostess)

Sécheresse

(sesh-ress)
noun, feminine

drought

If you were to sneak over to our backyard fence, part its curtain of faded jasmine, and look past a ditch full of wild fennel grown as tall as our older child, you'd spy our next-door *voisin* showering beneath the fiery heavens at daybreak, scrub-a-dub-dubbing right in the middle of his *potager*!

But you wouldn't see a steel nozzle above his head or an anti-skid mat beneath his feet. Only a sturdy kitchen stool separates him from the muddy ground below, with its neatly trellised vines—vines which are, oddly, bursting with fruit during this, *The Year of the Drought*....

There, amongst ripe red *tomates*, stands my eco-conscious neighbor, garden hose held high above his head. I see no shelves on which to set his shampoo (is that a vinegar rinse he is using?...they say old wine is good for both hair *and* plants!), and no modesty's-sake shower curtain protects him from this housewife-voyeur (hence those bright blue swim trunks). On closer look, there is a serene expression on the showerer's face, as water from the *tuyau* trickles over it, splashing and quenching the thirsty *légumes* beneath.

In this period of *sécheresse*, the municipal Powers That Be forbid us to water our gardens...*but no one said you couldn't wash yourself!* I watch as the shower water rains down over the would-be parched vegetables, and I am impressed with my neighbor's clever solution to irrigating his *jardin*.

"You ought to try it sometime!" the man in the blue swim trunks calls out. I freeze, as would any nosy neighbor who has been found out.

My cheeks turn as red as those well-watered tomatoes and I quickly release the jasmine, letting the floral curtain fall to a close.

French Vocabulary

le voisin, la voisine
neighbor

le potager
vegetable garden

la tomate
tomato

le tuyau (d'arrosage)
garden hose

un légume
vegetable

la sécheresse
drought

le jardin
garden

Crotte

(krot)
noun, feminine

doo-doo

THE FIRST TIME WE DINED TOGETHER, SHE REMARKED THAT I WAS STUFFY. Specifically, she said she had the impression that she had spent the evening with "*la Reine*." Her remarks struck me as ironic, for it was this woman and her upper-class status which had been so intimidating to me.

So when it was my turn to invite my neighbor and her husband for *le déjeuner*, I took care to appear more relaxed, *even though I was twice as nervous*, given her previous impression of me.

Stuffy? Perhaps my nerves were to blame, for we were dining at the home of a local personality. Yes, I must have been a little bit crisp as I carefully sat down on an elegant sofa and began to take in my surroundings. The home was filled with romantic statues and modern-art paintings; fresh flowers dressed every table.

I thought about what I had worn that evening: did my attire lead her to classify me as *coincée*? I'd worn a long skirt and a button-down *chemise* under a cardigan. She had worn leopard and those glittery stiletto heels....

This time I wore all black, mindful to *défaire* one more button on my blouse. Though I had upped my efforts to be cool, relaxed, and very un-*reine*-like, my neighbor (now wearing sequins for our lunch date) had another agenda.

From the kitchen, where I was serving up steaming bowls of pumpkin-and-chestnut soup (soup, a.k.a. "the peasants' meal"...no queen would serve that!), I heard the laughter. Maybe it had something to do with my cooking? I had been so nervous at the idea of serving my neighbor's husband, a renowned chef!

When I went out to see what was so amusing, I found my husband and the *invités* standing, their eyes watering, their sides splitting.

"What? What is so funny?"

My eyes scanned the living room for any "laughable" objects strewn about, *bricoles* or *bibelots* I had looked at so often that the novelty had worn off. I saw nothing *ridicule*. Next, I checked my clothes to see whether something had gone wrong during the dressing stage. That is when I noticed my blouse, which was tucked into my underwear.

My fashion gaffe wasn't in tucking a shirt into a *culotte* (people do this all the time—don't they?), but in wearing low-waisted pants. *Dumb, dumb, dumb!*

The good news was that I was looking as down-to-earth as ever! Just how much more relaxed could one get? Such a get-up might dethrone this so-called "queen" once and for all, or at the very least earn a few "graceless" points with the neighbor who thinks me so stuffy, so *reine*-like.

I soon realized that no one was looking at my underwear. All eyes were fixed to the floor. Curious, I followed my guests' gazes. That's when I saw IT. So dull. So deflated, So *dégoûtante!* A caramel-toned coil lying atop the tiled floor right next to the dining table.

Une crotte!

I stood staring at it, stunned. *Une crotte de chien?* But we don't have a dog....

Elbowed by the woman standing beside him, my husband spoke: "Kristi—*what is that?*" I looked to the others for an explanation. The blank looks I received only intensified my embarrassment. What happened next was the French version of The Twilight Zone.

Jean-Marc went over and picked up that *crotte!* Next, he handed it to my sequined guest, who then put it in her pocket....

That is when I realized I had been tricked—fooled by fake dog-doo, no less!

How to react? As dumbstruck as I was, I did not want to lose my new "unstuffy" status! I had worked so hard to dash any misconceptions! But I did not want my delayed response to condemn my neighbor, who I sensed did not mean any harm—*au contraire*—she had found in that classic gag what she felt to be a friendly icebreaker.

"Where can I get one of those?" I ventured, walking my stiletto-heeled guest to the door after lunch.

"Here. You can have it. It's yours!" my neighbor winked, patting me on the back, as pals do. It seemed I had somehow passed the test and, I hoped, found a new friend thanks to an old jest.

French Vocabulary

la reine
the queen

le déjeuner
lunch

coincé(e)
uptight

la chemise
shirt

défaire
to undo

un(e) invité(e)
a guest

une bricole
trinket

le bibelot
knickknack

ridicule
laughable

la culotte
underwear

dégoûtant(e)
disgusting

la crotte de chien
dog mess

au contraire
just the opposite

Béton

(bay-tohn)
noun, masculine

concrete

MY SON HAS MENTIONED WANTING TO BE A BAKER OR A CONSTRUCTION worker when he grows up, but I suspect his talent might lie in styling.

For the past year Max has been working hard at perfecting what I call *the gentleman's Mohawk*: "gentleman's," for the understated height of the hair (so subtle you could almost get away with it at the office or at school...if your mom weren't waiting by the front door each morning with the flat side of her hand ready to "mow" down your "hawk").

"It's called *une crête*," Max corrects me, "...*une crête iroquoise!*"

"OK, Max. That may be. But you aren't allowed to wear your hair like that to school. It isn't polite."

But wear his hair like that at home he does, so much so that he is running out of gel again.

"*Papa*," Max asks during the drive to school, "the next time you go to the supermarket can you get me the '*gel fixation béton*'?"

I can't help but laugh at what he has just requested: "concrete binding gel."

"Even if you spin on your head," Max insists, "your hair won't move—not one millimeter! My friend Lucas has the concrete gel and the last time he fell on his head *rien a bougé!* Not one hair went out of place!"

Recently I came across *une pub* for the gel my son requested. The ad suggests that with the help of this product, "*les cheveux sont durs comme du béton!*"

"Hard as concrete?..." I am reminded of Max's other when-I-grow-up wish: to work in masonry. Concrete...construction... Yes! I am finally seeing the subconscious connection! OK, in that case our son will need to rule out baking...or take the risk that his *pâtisseries* have the lightness or the flakiness of a cinder block!

French Vocabulary

une crête
comb, crest

une crête iroquoise
Mohawk (hair)

Papa
Dad

rien a bougé
nothing moved

la pub (publicité)
advertisement

les cheveux sont durs comme du béton
the hair is as hard as concrete

la pâtisserie
cake

$\mathscr{P}aresse$

(par-ess)
noun, feminine

laziness, idleness

BY THE TIME MY AUNT AND UNCLE FROM SAN FRANCISCO ARRIVED FOR A three-day visit, my home, my yard, my kids, my spouse, my dog and I, all in our Sunday best, were as put together as a family of paper dolls. All I needed to do for the next 72 hours was keep our cut-out cover-ups from blowing off: keep the kids from wiping their mouths with the backs of their hands, keep my husband from leaving the bathroom door open (while he occupied it!), keep the puppy from having indigestion and keep myself from feeling the need to explain the greasy fingerprints on the wall and the still-needs-fixin' front gate. It isn't often that I see my American family, so when they come to France I can't help but want them to believe that I've finally "arrived"...when the truth is I'm still zigzagging along *Le Grand Chemin de la Vie*.

Not 24 hours into last week's masquerade, my paper-thin façade was literally falling off. *It began with that monster spot in the back of my car....*

A little while back, one of our kids knocked over a bottle of water, soaking the back seat of our Citroën. When a large water stain

appeared, I dusted the *tache* with spot cleaner, only, when I went to remove the powder, the vacuum cleaner's motor went kaput. The spot, now larger and darker than before, remained. A few more weeks passed...and the tea-colored powder hardened!

The growing and darkening spot represented one great weakness: *la paresse*. That's right, SLOTH, or "the disinclination to work or exert oneself", a label I've been trying to tear off my person since whiling away many a childhood day in front of *I Love Lucy* or *The Bionic Woman* or *Pippi Longstocking* (while my funny, strong, and adventurous sister, Heidi, did the dishes).

But back to that monstrous *tache*. On the very first day of my family's visit, the spot was spotted! It happened when my uncle volunteered to take the back seat after I proposed a scenic drive. Noticing the blanket that covered the *siège arrière*, my curious uncle instinctively tugged at it, instantly revealing The Mutant Monster *Tache*—*and all of my flaws along with it*!

"You weren't supposed to see that!" I cried, blowing my own cover. "Everything was supposed to be perfect!"

My uncle was taken aback, either by the spot...or by my confession. After a moment, and in his best French and softest voice, he offered, "*Personne n'est parfaite.*"

After our excursion, by the time I had returned the car keys to the *armoire à clés*, my uncle had unbolted the back seat, pulled the entire *siège* unit out of the car, and hosed down its surface. After ten minutes and a little liquid laundry detergent and a scrub brush, the spot was completely gone! "*Ce n'était rien,*" my uncle reassured me.

Two days later I said goodbye to my aunt and uncle. It was while polishing the bathroom mirror that I noticed the apple spice lipstick stain on my cheek. "Stay the way you are," my aunt had said, planting the kiss. "Don't ever change."

True to character, I was a bit slack about removing that lipstick stain, and my aunt's apple spice kiss stayed on my cheek until it eventually wore itself off.

French Vocabulary

Le Grand Chemin de la Vie
Life's Great Path

la tache
stain, spot

le siège
seat

le siège arrière
back seat

Personne n'est parfaite
Nobody's perfect

une armoire à clés
key box

ce n'était rien
it was nothing, no big deal

Louper

(loo pay)
verb

to miss (a class...)

AFTER HIS HEARTY LUNCH OF *POULET RÔTI*, SPICY EGGPLANT *RATATOUILLE*, and rosemary potatoes (and seconds of all three!), I suspect that my son is brimming with health and not at all as sick as he claimed to be when the alarm clock rang this morning. (*"Aïe! J'ai mal au ventre!"* he complained. Feeling sympathetic, I let him stay home from school for the morning.)

"Well, well, Max, you certainly seem to be feeling better! Maybe I could take you to school now and you won't miss your afternoon classes?"

"Mommy," Max pleads, "I need a whole day off!"

"Well then, you'll have a lot of class work to catch up on, so don't come crying to me!"

Max offers me a disarming smile before asking what's for dessert. I bring out a bowl of aromatic *garriguettes*—strawberries so sweet you'd swear they were sugar cubes blushing in disguise. I pass Max the can of whipped cream, figuring that he might as well enjoy his sick day even if he is guilty.

As he eats, he reviews which classes he has missed:

J'ai loupé les maths...
J'ai loupé la musique...
J'ai loupé la téchno...

Listening to my son's losses, I try to balance the debit. Though Max missed math, music, and technology, he didn't miss doing the dishes (this, without my asking), he didn't miss making me a surprise cup of tea ("*C'est bien chaud!*" he announced, his shining eyes carefully steadied on the steamy surface of the tea lest it spill as he walked), and he didn't miss collecting a handful of roses (after he slipped out to the garden, scissors in hand). Finally, he didn't miss selecting a vase (our best coffee cup in the cupboard) and arranging the flowers into an attractive bouquet before delivering them to my desk. "For you, Mommy," he offered.

"*J'ai loupé un peu d'histoire.*" I missed a bit of history, too, my son admits as I poke my nose deep into a pink blossom.

Learning about another "louped" class, I feel slightly annoyed. Then I get to thinking about Max's history book and all the "important stuff" that is recorded inside for students to study and recall. Why shouldn't this moment, too, be memorized?

How unworthy of note one boy's stolen day may seem to historians, who will never document the sweetness of this tea, or record the gift of a tender heart.

French Vocabulary

le poulet rôti
rotisserie chicken

Aïe! J'ai mal au ventre!
Ow! I have a stomach ache

j'ai loupé les maths
I missed math

j'ai loupé la musique
I missed music

j'ai loupé la téchno (technologie)
I missed technology

c'est bien chaud
it's very hot

J'ai loupé un peu d'histoire
I missed a little bit of history

Conduire

(kohn-dweer)
verb

to drive

In the winter of 2001, I left work at the vineyard each night to drive myself to driving school, careful to take the back roads and to park several blocks from the *Auto-École Rivière*. Though I had driven for ten years in the States, and another six in France, I had failed to exchange my Arizona driver's license for a French one, having had two years to do so. Time and again, Jean-Marc assured me that I had the right to drive in France (convinced that my AAA International Driving Permit was enough, never mind the expiration date), until one day he realized that his wife was driving without insurance (!!!); that is, should she get into an accident, the insurance contract would be void ($$$) without her having a French *permis de conduire*.

Having spent weeknights at driving school, attending class with would-be motorists half my age, and having finally passed *l'épreuve théorique*, or written exam, in the town of Fréjus, I would soon be navigating the streets of Draguignan...with a stony-faced *inspecteur* seated beside me.

On exam day, I shared the test vehicle with a wide-eyed 18-year-old who had just been ordered to pull over and get out.

"Out! You are a danger to yourself and to others!" the *inspecteur* shouted. Seated in the back of the car, waiting my turn, I tried to understand just what my unfortunate classmate had done wrong, but was jolted out of my *pensées* when the inspector resumed his tirade.

"FAILED!" the *inspecteur* barked. He shouted a few more insults before the French kid got into the back of the car, at which point I was ordered into the driver's seat: "*A vous, madame!*"

"*Allez-y!*" the *inspecteur* commanded, checking his watch. I said a prayer to Saint Christopher, patron saint of safe travel (not knowing who the saint was for driver's-exam scoring), put on the left-turn signal, and drove out of the quiet neighborhood into the chaotic streets of Draguignan at rush hour.

"You don't need to be so obvious!" the inspector snapped when I threw my chin left after turn-signaling. Moments ago I'd signaled a right turn and thrown my chin over my right shoulder for good measure. We had been warned in driving school to exaggerate our gestures during testing to show the *inspecteur* that we were aware of those dangerous "*angles morts*" or blind spots. "*Et les vitesses!*" the inspector grumbled after I'd ground the gears once again. "Oh, but aren't cars *automatic* in America?!" he snickered.

Though I had been stick-shifting for sixteen years, seated next to the *inspecteur* I felt as though I were operating a vehicle for the first time.

Having completed the 20-minute *parcours* through the center of Draguignan, where the unpredictable French pedestrian is king and capable of jumping from sidewalk to street center in the blink of an eye, I followed the *inspecteur's* instructions, pulling up in front of the American cemetery, which seemed like a bad omen to me.

The *inspecteur* sat silently filling out paperwork, before announcing it was time to check my vision. He ordered me to read the sign across the street. Squinting my eyes, I began:

"World War II Rhone American Cemetery and Memor...".

Before I had even finished reading, the inspector scribbled something across the page, tore off the sheet, and mumbled "*Félicitations.*"

Ornery as he was, I had the urge to throw my arms around the *inspecteur* and plant a kiss beside his angry brow; only, the *commandant* was no longer facing me, but looking out over the quiet green fields dotted white with courage, lost in another place and time.

French Vocabulary

Auto-École Rivière
Riviera Driving School

le permis (m) de conduire
driver's license

l'inspecteur (l'inspectrice)
examiner

la pensée
thought

A vous, madame
Your turn, Madam

Et les vitesses!
And the gears!

le parcours
driving route

les félicitations (fpl)
congratulations

le commandant
captain

Conjoint

(kohn-zhwan)
noun, masculine

spouse

JUST OFF THE COAST OF BRITTANY, ON A SMALL ISLAND *HABITÉE* BY *GROISIL-lons* and teeming with French tourists on wobbly *bicyclettes*, there is a quaint port called Locmaria, where The Drunk Boat overlooks the bay at high tide (and low, for that matter, but for the purpose of this *conte* the *marée* shall be high, high as the curious individual bathing in its shallow waters)....

"Ah, nature fresh and free. Yes, freeeeeeeeeeeeee!"

I can just hear his French words echoing across the sandy beach, translating themselves in midair before reaching The Drunk Boat bar on the boardwalk above, near to which a red-faced tourist stands hesitant. Red-faced, not because she is a native of the desert, which she is, but because her Frenchman (*he who bathes in shallow waters*) has been caught, once again, *en flagrant délit* with *Dame Nature*. Yes, caught red-handed (and mud-in-the-hand) as you will soon discover.

It isn't the first time he has been found courting *La Dame*; take him to the powdery depths of the canyon at Roussillon, and he'll brush red and yellow ochre across his stubbled face. "A tradition," he explains (the earth-smearing, not the stubble). Bring him to a

crowded beach in his beloved Marseilles, and he will inhale the salty waters beyond (via a noisy nose gargle). "Good for the sinuses," he exclaims. Cart him off to the wild *garrigue* and he will begin chewing on the local herbs (good for the gums, I wonder?). Go where he may, he will find a way to press the earth unto himself. He's *Monsieur Nature*.

Back at the bay in Locmaria, it is another day in Paradise for Monsieur Nature, who can be found applying mud to his person—sloshing it on from neck to knee—only, he calls the sludge "*vase*" (pronouncing it "vaz," as if a neat word would render his act less, well, *filthy*).

Standing knee-deep in the shimmering ocean, he scoops up the smelly *vase*, slops it on his arms and across his chest before a vigorous scrub-down. He works the mud, oblivious to the audience now gathering before him: there are the seagulls, beady eyes bulging, and the little crabs looking on, astonished, and even the mussels—clinging to a nearby rock—have opened their shells for a look-see. "Get a load of this," they clatter, their long, salmon-colored tongues wagging.

This, dear reader, is my mud-faced *conjoint* and that curious behavior of his, in a clamshell, is the difference between him and me; the difference, I now realize, between really living life and poetically lusting after it from the boardwalk above.

French Vocabulary

habitée (habiter)
inhabited

les Groisillons
inhabitants of the Island of Groix

la bicyclette
bicycle

The Drunk Boat (Le Bateau Ivre)
the name of a bar along the boardwalk

le conte
tale, story

la marée
tide

pris en flagrant délit
caught in the act

la Dame Nature
Mother Nature

la garrigue
wild Mediterranean scrubland

la vase
sludge, mud

le conjoint, la conjointe
spouse

Pantoufle

(pahn-too-fle)
noun, feminine

slipper

THE MAN IN LINE IN FRONT OF ME WORE *PANTOUFLES* TWO SIZES TOO SMALL. His swollen calves, riddled with eczema, hung over his ankles, which disappeared into his shrunken slippers. As usual, he wore sweatpants that rose mid-calf.

I often see the man in *pantoufles* hanging out of a village *poubelle*. He is passionate about garbage and is forever reaching for it. His backside, with the vertical line peeking out from the center of his waistband, is a familiar sight in our village. When he isn't dangling (and *flashing*) from a trash barrel, he is hunched over, collecting litter from the street, careful to put the waste where it belongs. We have a tidy village thanks to this man, who appears to both love and abhor trash.

Standing in line at the *Crédit Agricole*, the man wearing *pantoufles* waited for his turn to visit the bank teller. He had that same blank look on his face, the one he wears while hunting for garbage: expressionless, transfixed by trash—or troubled by it, you never know.

From behind the counter, the pretty *guichetière* inquired:

"How much today, Jean-Pierre?"

J.-P. stepped forward and replied, "*Vingt euros.*"

"*Il n'y a pas.* You don't have that much," the teller said. "How about fifteen?"

Jean-Pierre nodded, fixing his eyes on a ballpoint pen chained to the *comptoir*.

"Here you are. And don't spend it all at the *Bar des Sports*, okay?"

Jean-Pierre remained unresponsive to the *guichetière's* charm and humor. Though the carefree cashier and the catatonic garbage-picker had this same exchange every day, I stood there, ill at ease about over-hearing the limits of J.-P.'s fortune. Not that I didn't know even more about him—and his family (everyone knows everything about every-body in this village. *Or so they like to think they do*).

Take, for example, J.-P.'s sister, Agnès, who hangs out the clothes to dry along their apartment's tiny 2nd-floor balcony. *She does house-work in her underwear.* The only time she is dressed is in the winter or when she walks her dilapidated dog. She has the same corpulent frame as her brother and looks identical to him; only, she wears teal-green eye shadow, caked black mascara and red lipstick when she drinks. Drunk or sober, her unbrushed hair is a *nid d'oiseau.*

When she's not hanging out clothes, Agnès can be heard a kilo-meter away, barking orders to their elderly mother.

"*J'en ai marre! Mange! Mange!* I'm fed up! Eat! Eat!" she shouts, wav-ing a spoon before her mother.

My own mom, Jules, who lived for a while in a third-floor studio across the street from Jean-Pierre and his family, encouraged me not to be so quick to judge Agnès (pronounced ON-yes).

"She has so many worries," Mom explained. "Poor thing. She has to spoon-feed her mother, who sits there, mouth clamped shut, stub-born as can be. When she does get a spoonful in, her mother just spits it right back out! Then she's got all that laundry. She never stops!"

I tried not to judge Agnès, but I did find myself avoiding her, and I crossed the street at the sight of her and her *porto*-enflamed cheeks. Something about her seemed *déséquilibrée*.

One day, while walking to my mom's studio, I saw Agnès slumped over her doorstep. I noticed she was dressed. From her eyes poured two black rivers, down her face, across her red lips and onto her thin, soiled shirt. My mom sat next to Agnès, her arm around the sad woman's shoulder. In front of the women there was a flurry of French paramedics, beyond, a narrow stretcher covered with a long white sheet. My eyes locked on the bundle in the center, beneath *le drap blanc*.

That evening I saw Agnès' brother snapping up litter from the uneven cobblestone paths of our village. His pants were on straight, and the unsightly crack had disappeared. Gone were his predictable *pantoufles*. He wore white, canvas tennis shoes, his puffy heels hanging out the back. His face remained expressionless, though his lips sunk a bit at each end. His hair was combed, parted. Just like the garbage collector's shoes, the village was pristine the night they carried Agnès's and Jean-Pierre's mother away.

The trash man may never understand the beautiful bank teller's humor, but Life's comedy is something he knows: as with the never-ending reach of litter, the trick is to keep moving, to keep after it. Life, that is.

French Vocabulary

la pantoufle
house slippers

la poubelle
garbage can

le Crédit Agricole
one of the large retail banking groups in France

la guichetière
the bank teller

vingt euros
twenty euros

le comptoir
counter

le nid d'oiseau
bird's nest

déséquilibré
unbalanced

le drap blanc
white sheet

Foi

(fwa)
noun, feminine

faith

MY DAUGHTER SAYS THAT BOOKS ARE LIKE CIGARETTES, *UNE MAUVAISE HABI-tude*, and would I please put the reading aside for one night?

"Of course, Sweetheart," I promise, returning the book to its shelf. Is that a tremble in my arm? Sweat on my brow?

"And the *cahiers* and the pens—put them away, too!" Jackie insists.

My head starts to pound and the twitching begins. I leave my hard- and my soft-bound drugs, feeling the first symptoms of withdrawal as I walk away from words. I tell my daughter that I got the habit from her Mexican grandmother, Hoolia, and that one day she, too, will need a paper-and-pen fix. It runs in the family like flat hair and latent fury.

I don't tell my daughter that her Mexican grandmother, Jules, is really American, but leave it as Jackie's told it time and again. It is her story and not mine, and she gets that storytelling gene from Hoolia, or Julia—*make that "Jules"*.

At the dinner table, Jackie asks, "Why does Grandma Jules dress up for dinner?"

I sit there in my felt slippers and pajamas, thinking up an answer. "Because people like to look at pretty things when they eat, and don't we love looking at Grandma Jules?" My daughter agrees.

When Jackie says, "Let's do like Grandma Jules!" I prepare to get up, walk to the powder room, and put on some *rouge à lèvres*. Instead, my daughter reaches for my hand, closes her eyes and says:

"Dear Lord, thank you for this food."

It is no thanks to me, nose deep in a book, fingers curled around another *cartouche*, that my daughter learned to pray. But tonight we'll take Hoolia's example, and hope that—like fury and fine hair—faith runs in this family…if not always in stride.

French Vocabulary

une mauvaise habitude
a bad habit

le cahier
notebook

une cartouche
(ink) cartridge
(refill for ball-point pens)

le rouge à lèvres
lipstick

s'Occuper

(so-kew-pay)
verb

to keep oneself busy

Italian Josephine made homemade pizza the size of a hamburger patty, only there wasn't any *viande*, just a bony anchovy and a meaty olive or two. When she had the energy, she delivered her Italian pies and stayed to watch you enjoy them. And she never charged.

"*Ça m'occupe.*" It keeps me busy, she would say, simply. As I ate, she would sit facing me with her cane, her knitted shawl, and her buckled shoes, and reminisce about an American friend, whose name she shared, and the adventures they had back in the '50s along the Côte d'Azur, when one ran an Italian *épicerie* and the other ran away from Paris. I listened, but mostly I studied Josey, whose dark eyes, once dull, now sparkled.

The last time Josephine showed up at my door with one of her trademark mini pizzas, she was carrying a black-and-white photograph.

"I have something to show you," she said. We sat at the table, I in my one-size-fits-all dress (weeks away from giving birth to my second child) and Josey with her shawl and cane and buckled shoes, the black-and-white photo between us. The scratched and faded image revealed the two glowing Josephines: one "*café*," the other "*au lait.*"

The women were dressed in satin kimonos and holding umbrellas, smiles as big as the complicity they shared. I studied the old photo from afar when suddenly my Josey mentioned that her friend loved to sing and dance....

Sing. Dance. *Josephine!* That's when I grabbed the photo from the table and viewed, up close, the veritable, the one and only *Josephine Baker*—the celebrated American *danseuse* (and sometime secret agent) known to appear at the Paris *Folies* in nothing more than a *jupe* made of bananas, her pet leopard, Chiquita, in tow.

My excitement was cut short when Josey told me that she was moving to Saint-Raphaël, that her daughter could no longer look after her here in Saint-Maximin. I quietly set down the photo and looked at my friend as a lump formed in my throat. *C'est toujours comme ça*, I thought bitterly. Just when you meet someone—*the kind of person you can just sit with and say nothing to and not feel awkward, the kind who makes a little pizza pie for you because they are thinking of you in your absence*—they up and move to a faraway city!

Before Josephine left, she pushed the photo across the table. *"C'est pour toi,"* she said in her soft voice. I tried to tell her that I could not accept her photo, that she should keep it, but she insisted.

I couldn't take Josey's only photo of her with her legendary friend...unless...*unless it wasn't the only one?* Perhaps there were others? Yes! There must be others of those "girls" in the good ol' days—other snapshots—*with leopards and banana skirts and maybe a feather boa or two!*

I watched as my Josey padded out the door, little steps with her big-buckle shoes. So fragile, she seemed, that you might have taken her for a broken-winged bird, but for the leopard-printed tracks in her wake.

French Vocabulary

la viande
meat

l'épicerie (f)
grocer's

le café
coffee

au lait
with milk

la danseuse (le danseur)
dancer

Folies
Les Folies Bergères
(famous music hall in Paris)

la jupe
skirt

c'est toujours comme ça
it is always that way

c'est pour toi
it's for you

Ceinture de sécurité

(sen-tewr)
noun, feminine

seat belt

Go back in time with me now, if you will, to the historic town of St. Maximin, where visitors from all over the world come to see the purported relics of Mary Magdalene (behind a thick glass encasement in the town's basilica).

The year is 1998 and the tree-lined parking lot in front of our centuries-old village home is *complet*. All fourteen parking spaces have been claimed. I am about to make one Frenchman's day by freeing *une place*—just as soon as I can wrestle my one- and three-year-olds into their car seats!

While I fasten Jackie's seatbelt, Max hums, pulls at my hair, or points to the pigeons in the dilapidated square. Beneath the campanile, which hasn't announced the hour in years, Madame A is scattering baguette crumbs again. If she keeps this up, there will be more birds in this village than beret-sporting Frenchmen! Maybe that's her plan?

I hear a familiar voice and I look up, past the car seat, to see Monsieur B, my other neighbor, shaking his head. "*Elle est complètement dingue!*" he mumbles, shaking his head at our neighbor. Perched there

on the curb in front of *les pompes funèbres*, Monsieur looks as old as Mary Magdalene.

Monsieur B hates it when Madame feeds the pigeons. *"C'est sale!"* he complains, pointing to the *crotte*-lined curb. I sidestep the pigeon droppings on my way around the car. Time to buckle in Max, now that his sister is secure in her car seat.

"Mommy's going to put YOUR *ceinture* on now," I explain. Max stops humming and releases another lock of my hair. His eyes leave the pigeons to refocus on my still-pursed lips. Next, his little voice insists, "SEN-tewr, *maman!* SEN-tewr!"

Ah, bon? It seems I am mispronouncing again. I see my son point to my lips as he opens his own mouth to demonstrate the correct sound.

The car behind me begins to honk. I signal *un instant* to the impatient driver, who is still waiting for our parking spot. Turning back to my son, I repeat the word as my three-year-old has instructed.

"SEN... SEN-tewr..." Yes! I now hear the difference: SEN—like century, and not SAHN, like sonnet.

"Voilà, maman!" the little voice confirms.

With that, Max resumes his humming, I run around the car (past the other driver, who flails his arms in exasperation), Madame A tosses more breadcrumbs, Monsieur B shakes his head, and the pigeons continue to populate the village square as life goes on in the little French town of St. Maximin.

French Vocabulary

complet
full

une place
a spot (parking place)

Elle est complètement dingue!
She is absolutely nuts!

pompes funèbres (fpl)
funeral home

c'est sale
it's dirty

la crotte
droppings

la ceinture
seatbelt

Ah, bon?
Oh, really?

voilà, maman
there you have it, mommy

Attentionné

(ah-tahn-syon-ay)

thoughtful, attentive

WHEN MY FATHER RETURNED HOME TO IDAHO FROM FRANCE, HE HAD A few foreign banknotes left over from his trip. Thoughtfully, he tucked the paper euros into a book and sent the money safely to me.

When the slim volume arrived, I admired its gold cover... until I remembered the gift inside (and dived in)!

The cash lasted only seconds in my hand before my son walked into the room, his sleeves inching up his arms, over his growing wrists....

And so I put the *pognon* into my pocket, the kids into the car, and the cash into two new winter coats. The children warm and snug, I returned home from the store to feel the chill of *Hiver's* approach.

Shivering, I reopened my father's book and the warmth of his words enveloped me.

(My father's inscription read: "I'm very proud of you. Love, Dad.")

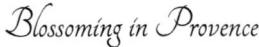

French Vocabulary

le pognon
cash, dough

l'hiver (m)
winter

NOTE: The book my father sent me was the sentimental short story *The Snow Goose*, by Paul Gallico.

Coquille

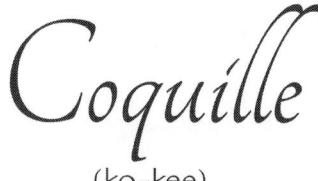

(ko-kee)
noun, feminine

shell

WHEN I AM OLD AND WRINKLED—WELL INTO THE *TROISIÈME ÂGE*—I WANT to race along the shores of Brittany on my *Mobylette,* that most groovy of French bikes with an engine!

I want to be an eccentric *vieille dame.* I don't want to care about what anyone thinks, as long as I am not imposing myself on their *philosophie de vie.* I'll ride my old bike along the seashore. I'll wear black goggles and wrap a long wool scarf, in orange *potiron,* around my neck. Off I'll fly, scarf ends flowing in the wind.

I'll let go of the pedals, WHEEEEEEEEE...and sing a song by Yves Montand—or a tune from *Les Misérables*—depending on my mood.

I'll pack a picnic with all my *favoris.* Inside the *panier* there'll be boiled eggs, *anchoïade, Gratin Dauphinois,* pungent cheese, a soft baguette and a flask of Earl Grey. There'll be tangerines to eat and a few squares of dark chocolate.

I'll gather delicate *coquilles* from the foamy seashore and tie them to my shoes. You'll hear the jingle of seashells when I pedal by.

My voice will be agreeably hoarse, not from les *Gauloises* or *le vin* but from whistling all the day long—a habit I'll have picked up at

the beginning of the century, when a certain Frenchwoman cautioned: "*Les femmes ne sifflent pas!* Women don't whistle!" That's when I puckered up and blew another tune...and another...and then one more!

I hope to have a dear old friend, one who is much more *excentrique* than I. She'll dye her white hair *rouge vif* or *aubergine*. We'll *tchatche* about the current generation and how people need to loosen up and *profiter un peu de la vie*, enjoy life a little, like us.

I'll say, "*Pépé—les oursins!*" and my old man will return from the rocky pier where he has spent the morning hunting sea urchins. When he cracks open their *coquilles*, revealing the mousse-like orange roe, I will remember that real treasures don't come with a price tag.

I want to live near the seagulls so that I may slumber beneath their cries and wake up to the whoosh of the sea. I'll push myself to a stand, smooth back my white locks, adjust a faux tortoiseshell comb, and say "*Dieu merci!*" for another day.

Before I tuck myself into bed at night I will, once again, empty *mes coquilles* into an old metal cookie tin, a treasure from long ago. Looking over to my seashells, I will give thanks: my cherished, tired tin runneth over.

French Vocabulary

le troisième âge
retirement

Mobylette
a particular model of moped

une vieille dame
a venerable lady

une philosophie (f) de vie
a life philosophy

orange potiron
pumpkin orange

favori(te)
favorite

un panier
a basket

l'anchoïade (m)
anchovy purée mixed with olive oil

un Gratin Dauphinois
a potato casserole with milk, butter and cheese

une coquille
a shell

la Gauloise
brand of cigarettes

le vin
wine

excentrique
eccentric

rouge vif
bright red

aubergine
eggplant purple

tchatcher
to chat (away)

le pépé
grandpa

un oursin
a sea urchin

Dieu merci
Thank God

Lumière

(loo-mee-air)
noun, feminine

light

THE MEMORY OF THAT MIDSUMMER NIGHT IS QUICKLY FADING AND MY mind's eye must squint for the scene to come into view again, fragmented and incomplete.

I can just see the subject in the foreground and how the light playing upon him, along with the quiet night, made for a breathtaking still life.

Just what shade of orange was it washing over the plateaus along the landscape of his back? Tangerine comes to mind.

I should have missed the color—sunburst orange?—what with the fine-lined paperback before me, stealing my vision.

It was the rustling leaves that beckoned, that had my eyes leaving the page to refocus on the chestnut tree outside and to the blue cypress hedge below before returning to the room, riding the night's breeze, to my husband slumbering beside me.

My mind watches now as the street light throws an orangey glow over the outspoken curves of his back. There, between darkness and *lumière*, I glimpse the drama of here and now.

I flip a page in the paperback...only to pause before the text: do the words that I am reading have as much mystery, beauty, or meaning? I close my book and read the moment instead.

Un mot de Jean-Marc...

ALORS QUE JE TRIAIS RÉCEMMENT DE VIEUX PAPIERS, JE SUIS TOMBÉ SUR les magnifiques lettres que Kristi m'a écrit il ya 20 ans, alors que nous venions juste de nous connaître. Son talent d'écriture était déjà là, mais la véritable raison de son succès est qu'elle a durement travaillé ce don tous les jours.

En fait, le français est la principale raison qui fait que Kristi est devenue écrivaine. Alors qu'elle appréciait déjà d'apprendre cette langue dans son université de l'Arizona, elle a fait un programme d'échange en France avec une escapade romantique à Aix en Provence....

Un peu plus tard, elle m'a marié et nous a donné deux beaux enfants. Comme elle était souvent frustrée d'élever deux enfants dans une culture et une langue étrangères, elle a commencé à écrire à ses proches sur sa vie familiale d'expatriée...avec ses joies et ses peines. Ceci, non seulement l'a aidé à évacuer ces difficultés, mais lui a donné confiance en son écriture. French Word A Day est né comme ça.

Aujourd'hui, je suis fier de voir tout ce qu'elle a accompli jusqu'ici et je suis sûr qu'elle ne dévoile que la partie visible de l'iceberg de son talent. Et, outre la joie qu'elle donne à ses lecteurs trois fois par semaine, ses vignettes sont à jamais un trésor éternel de notre histoire familiale.

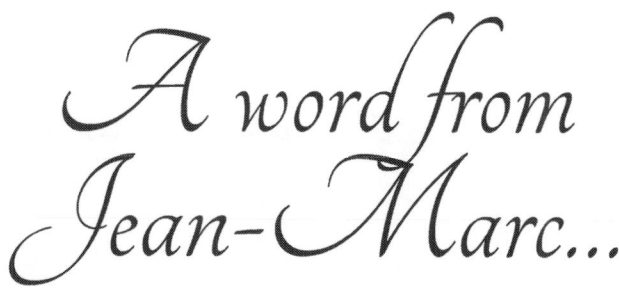

A word from Jean-Marc...

WHILE I WAS RECENTLY SORTING OLD PAPERS, I CAME ACROSS THE BEAUTIFUL letters that Kristi wrote me 20 years ago when we started to date. Her writing talent was already there, but the reason for her success is that she has been developing this gift by working hard every day.

In fact, French is the main reason Kristi has become a writer. As she was enjoying learning this language at her university, in Arizona, she did an exchange program in France, with a romantic getaway to Aix-en-Provence....

A couple of years later, she married me and gave us two beautiful children. As she was struggling with culture and language issues while raising two kids, she started to write about her daily expat life. This not only helped her to let go of some frustrations but gave her confidence in her writing. French Word-A-Day was born like that.

Today, I am proud to see all that she has accomplished so far, and I am sure that she is only showing the tip of the iceberg regarding her talent. Most of all, besides the joy she gives her readers, her vignettes will be forever a beautiful memory of our family life.

These stories continue at
www.French-Word-A-Day.com

"Take a great trip with a memorable travel book ...
and lose yourself in the South of France."

REAL SIMPLE

"Espinasse recounts her adventures with honesty and humor,
never afraid to have a good laugh at her own expense.
With its innovative and entertaining way of teaching the finer
points of French, Espinasse's memoir will be popular with
travelers and expats alike."

PUBLISHERS WEEKLY

"Charming."

LIBRARY JOURNAL

Read Kristin's book

Words in a French Life

"WHEN FALL BREAK, OR *LES VACANCES DE LA TOUSSAINT*, ARRIVED, I JOINED A classmate and boarded an all-night train. Stepping off the platform in Aix-en-Provence, I knew instantly that the south of France was where I wanted to be—forever. I stood in awe before the puzzle-skinned plane trees that lined an ancient cobblestone boulevard, the lively cafés that spilled out onto the bustling sidewalks, and the moss-covered fountains that acted as commas along an exclamation-packed boulevard.

After less than three months in Lille, fall semester ended and it was time to return home to the desert. While my classmates headed back to Arizona, I found a way to stay on in France, with permission from the department adviser to do an independent study. In exchange for college credit, I wrote about French culture as I had experienced it in Lille and in my new town, Aix, where I had moved. I was just buying time; for what, I did not know. What was sure was that I did not want to leave France. Not yet...."

EXCERPT FROM WORDS IN A FRENCH LIFE

Available at amazon.com, or ask your local book store to order it.

Notes

Notes

Notes

_____

_____

_____

_____

_____

_____

_____

_____

_____

_____

_____

_____

_____

_____

_____

_____

_____

_____

_____

Notes

12694563R00097

Made in the USA
Lexington, KY
22 December 2011